IT'S NEVER TOO LATE
TO PLAY PIANO

A learn-as-you-play tutor

P A M E L A   W E D G W O O D

© 1993 by Faber Music Ltd
First published in 1993 by Faber Music Ltd
3 Queen Square London WC1N 3AU
Music and text set by Ternary Graphics
Design by Lynette Williamson
Cover design by Shirley Tucker
Cartoons © 1993 by John Levers
Printed in England

FABER *ff* MUSIC

For Your Reference

Music depends on **rhythm** (time) and pitch.

Counting the Time

Note values

o = semibreve or whole note = 4 counts

𝅗𝅥 = minim or half note = 2 counts

♩ = crotchet or quarter note = 1 count

♪ = quaver or eighth note = ½ count

♬ = semiquaver or sixteenth note = ¼ count

Music is divided up by bar-lines. The space between the lines is called a bar, or measure.

bar   bar-line   double bar-line at end

Time values

A time-signature is placed at the beginning of a piece of music to tell you how many counts (beats) there are in each bar. The top figure tells you how many beats in the bar. The bottom figure tells you the value of those beats.

These are the simplest and most commonly-used time-signatures:

$\frac{4}{4}$ = 4 crotchet/quarter note (1-beat) notes to the bar

$\frac{3}{4}$ = 3 crotchets to the bar $\frac{2}{4}$ = 2 crotchets to the bar

Clap these rhythms, keeping a steady beat:

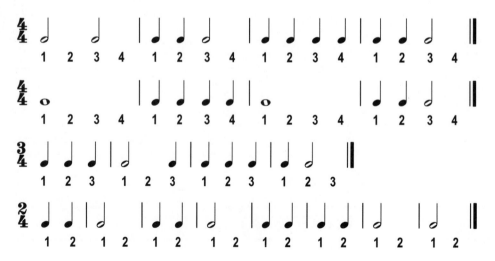

To show their **pitch**, notes are written on a five-line **stave**:

Notes are written
on the **lines**

or in the **spaces**

If we use notes that go above or below the stave, we add extra short lines, called **ledger lines**

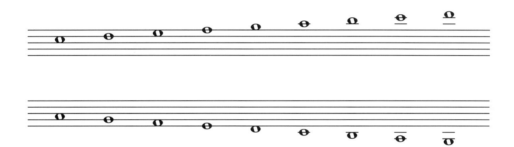

Nearly all keyboard music uses two staves, the upper one for the **right hand** and the lower one for the **left hand**.

Each stave has a **clef** at the beginning, to fix the pitch of the notes.

For high notes we use the treble clef:

and for low notes we use the bass clef:

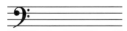

Mostly you will find the right hand playing in the treble clef and the left hand in the bass clef.

Introducing the 'It's Never Too Late' gang:

Hot Fingers   **Melody**   **Play-it-Again Sam**

How to sit at the keyboard

Always make sure you are sitting in the **middle** of the keyboard. Use an adjustable stool if possible, to find the most comfortable height.

Sit with your back straight, shoulders in a relaxed position.

Keep your fingers rounded. Imagine you are holding a ball in each hand. Fingers curved, wrists level with your arm.

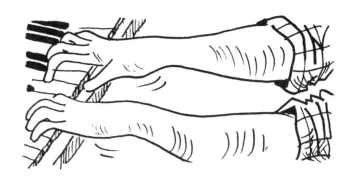

Keep your feet firmly on the ground!

The Keyboard

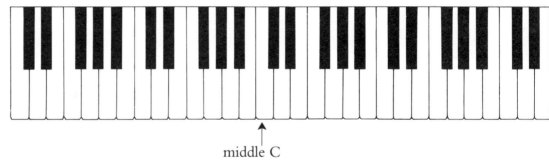

middle C

The keyboard has groups of black and white notes, which form a repeating pattern. The **white notes** are named after the first seven letters of the alphabet: A B C D E F G

Can you find all the C's on the keyboard?

Middle C is the C closest to the centre of the keyboard. On the stave, Middle C has its own line. In the Treble Clef, it looks like this:

Play Middle C with the **thumb** (1) of your right hand:

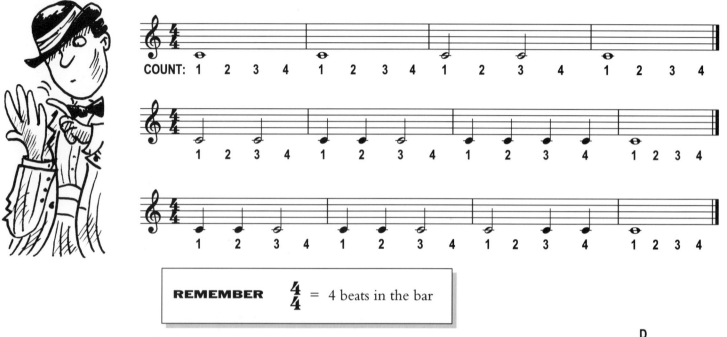

COUNT: 1 2 3 4 1 2 3 4 1 2 3 4 1 2 3 4

1 2 3 4 1 2 3 4 1 2 3 4 1 2 3 4

1 2 3 4 1 2 3 4 1 2 3 4 1 2 3 4

| REMEMBER | $\frac{4}{4}$ | = 4 beats in the bar |

New Note D

Use your 2nd finger to play D

COUNT: 1 2 3 4 1 2 3 4 1 2 3 4 1 2 3 4

Mix 'em up!

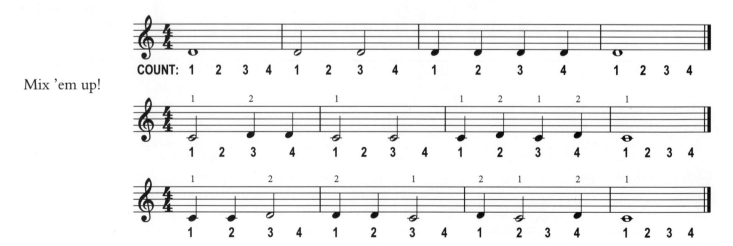

1 2 3 4 1 2 3 4 1 2 3 4 1 2 3 4

1 2 3 4 1 2 3 4 1 2 3 4 1 2 3 4

New Notes E and F

Use your 3rd and 4th fingers to play E and F

During the next exercise, say the **note names** out loud!

4-note Tango

New Note G

Use your 5th finger

Strengthening your 4th and 5th fingers

Look, no fingerings!

Name the notes – **play** and **say**

Go tell Aunt Nancy

Trad.

Part of the Vesper Hymn

Russian Air

Repeat

Almost Frère Jacques

Trad. French

Left Hand

Your Left Hand mostly plays in the Bass Clef.

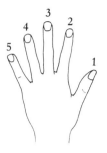

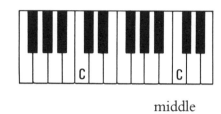

middle

Finding Lower C – use your 5th finger

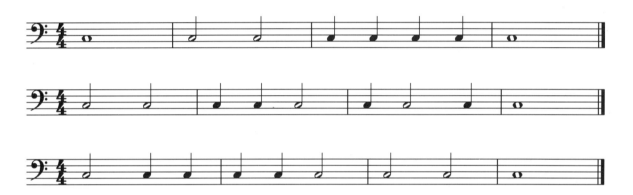

Lower D

middle

use your 4th finger

Mix'em up!

10

New Notes E and F

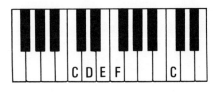

middle

use your 3rd and 2nd fingers

Walking that bass

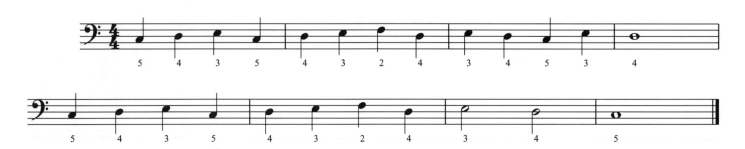

Finger strengtheners

Now repeat this exercise using any three next-door notes:

New note G

Play and **say**!

Look, no fingering!

Hymn

Far away

Trad.

Three very blind mice

Trad.

Melody's First Quick Quiz

How many counts on this note ? ♩

What are these lines called? ‖

How many counts on this note? 𝅝

What does 4/4 mean?

What is this sign called? 𝄞

What words do these notes make?

C major position

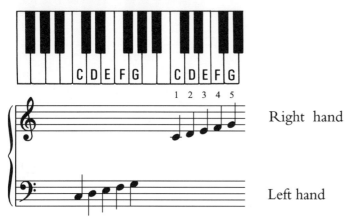

Right hand

Left hand

REMINDERS AND USEFUL TIPS

1. Clap and count the rhythm aloud. Name the notes.
2. Find the correct position for both hands.
3. Try to keep your eyes on the music while playing.

Hot Fingers 1

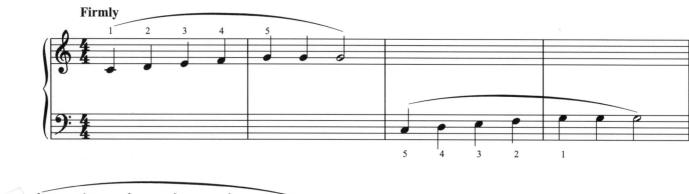

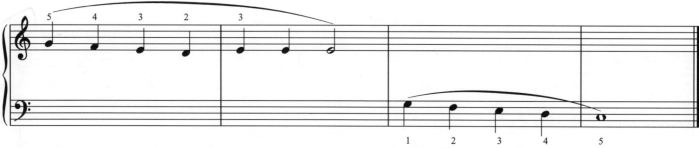

When you use both hands together, the treble and bass staves are joined by a **brace**:

brace →

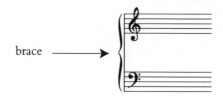

Hot Fingers 2

Hot Fingers Together for the First Time!

Hot Fingers Together Again!

Tunes you may know

Jingle Bells

Good King Wenceslas

Dotted notes

A dot makes a note work **overtime** – time-and-a-half, in fact.

𝅗𝅥. = 𝅗𝅥 + ♩ (dotted minim/half note – 3 counts in all)

𝅝. = 𝅝 + 𝅗𝅥 (dotted semibreve/whole note – 6 counts in all)

Play-it-Again Sam's Working Dots Test

Clap the following rhythmic exercises:

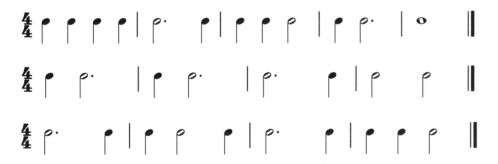

Melody's Second Quick Quiz

 = how many beats?

How many ♩ in a 𝅝?

What does **2/4** mean?

Name these notes:

UNIT FOUR

Rests

Rests indicate a gap in music, where the hand has a rest for a number of beats.

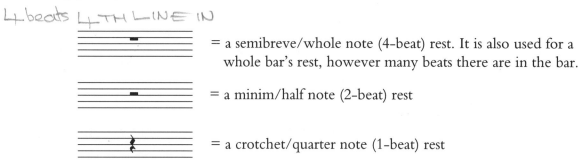

4 beats 4TH LINE IN

= a semibreve/whole note (4-beat) rest. It is also used for a whole bar's rest, however many beats there are in the bar.

= a minim/half note (2-beat) rest

= a crotchet/quarter note (1-beat) rest

Restercises

Practise and **count aloud**

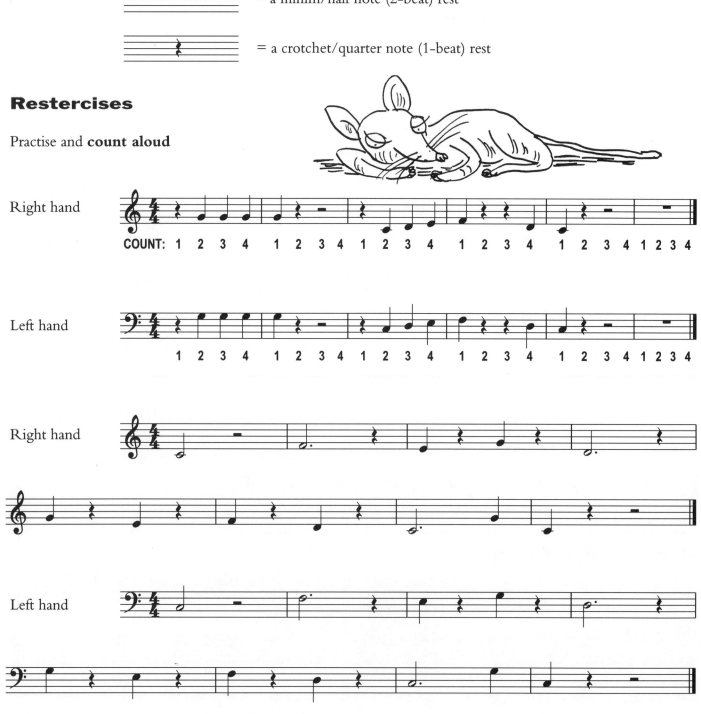

Three Resting Mice

REMEMBER $\frac{2}{4}$ = 2 x 1-beat notes to the bar

Rest awhile

Not fast

USEFUL TIP   Practise hands separately at first!

Togetherness

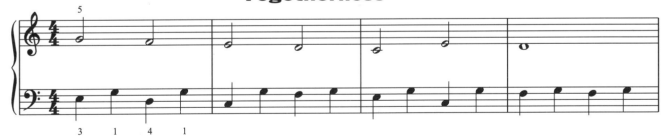

18

Tied notes

To make long notes we can join notes together with a tie

hold for 6 beats

hold for 8 beats

hold for 5 beats

Try these exercises:

All Tied Up!

COUNT: 1 2 3 4 | 1 2 3 4 | 1 2 3 4 | 1 2 3 4 | 1 2 3 4 | 1 2 3 4

Day Dream

Quick March

3/4 time (3 1-beat notes to the bar/measure)

Tap hands together

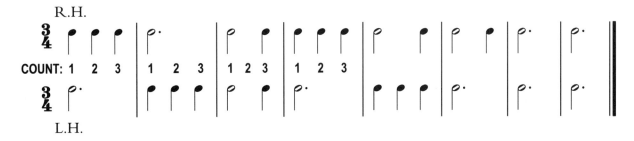

Clapping in **3/4** time

Adding a rest in **3/4** time

REMINDER ═══ is a whole bar's rest, even in **3/4** time!

Restercises

Togetherness 1

Waltz time

Togetherness 2

Tunes you may know

Summer Goodbye

German Drinking Song

Melody's Third Quick Quiz

How many counts on this note?

How many counts on this rest?

Name this sign?

How many ♩ in a ♩ ?

Name the notes **quickly**

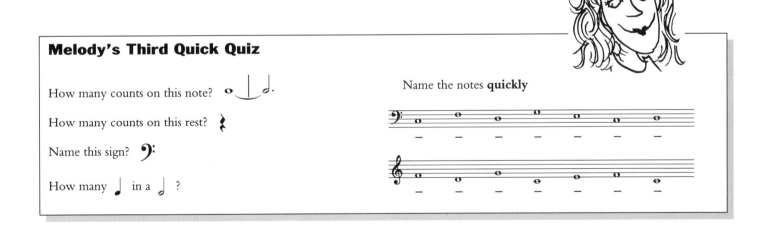

Upbeats

Notes that come before the first full bar/measure of a piece are called **Upbeats**. The time-value of the upbeat is usually taken away from the last bar, leaving it incomplete.

Examples

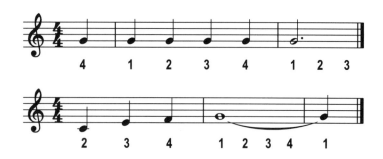

When the Saints Go Marching In

Signs and Terms

f	*forte* play loud		*pp*	*pianissimo* play very softly indeed
ff	*fortissimo* play very loud indeed		*mp*	*mezzo-piano* play moderately softly
mf	*mezzo-forte* play moderately loud	▷	*crescendo (cresc.)* gradually getting louder
p	*piano* play softly	◁	*decrescendo* or *diminuendo (dim.)* gradually getting softer

is called a **quaver** (eighth note), worth ½ a count. Two quavers look like this when joined together:

(= 1 count)

Play-it-Again Sam Rhythms

Clap and Say:

REMINDER	A dot makes a note work **overtime** – time-and-a-half
	$\bullet\, = \; 1 + ½ = 1½$ counts

Hot Fingers

Try each hand separately – then together

Quavering

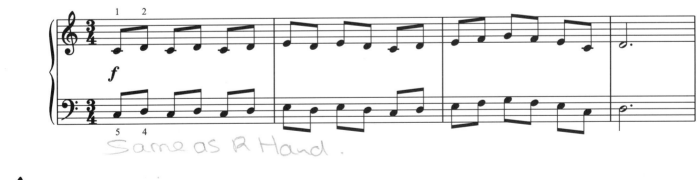

Same as R Hand.

Get those fingers moving!

Move 'em Fast

Play-it-Again Sam's Dotty Rhythm Tests

Clap, then **play**

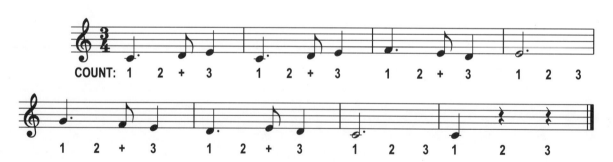

Nearly a 'Queen'

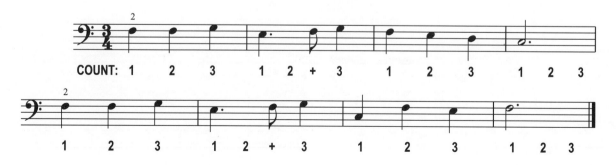

Play separate hands, then together:

Theme (from Sonata in A, K.331)

Mozart, arr. PW

Light and Shade

PW

Primary chords in the key of C major

A scale consists of a series of notes played consecutively, usually spanning at least one octave (eight notes)

Here is the scale of C major:

A chord consists of two or more notes played simultaneously. Chords built on the 1st, 4th and 5th notes of the scale are called **Primary Chords**.

In C major:

Chord I (C) uses the notes C E G
Chord IV (F) uses the notes F A C
Chord V^7 (G^7) uses the notes G B D F (the seventh note up from G)

Here is the scale of C major in the bass clef.
Play chords I, IV and V^7 based on C, F and G.

Let's look at the C chord and the G7 chord in the bass clef. To make the G7 chord easier to play we can leave out one note (D) and move the others around:

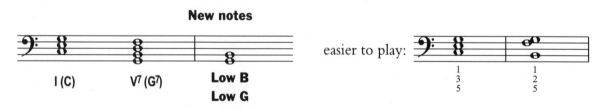

Hot Chord Warm-Up

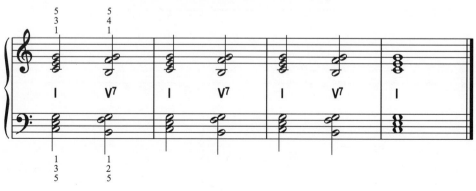

A tune you may know

Ode to Joy (Theme from Symphony No.9)

Watch the expression marks!

Play-it-Again Sam's Going As Fast As You Can Song

March

PW

Terms connected with speed

Moderato – moderately

Allegro – fast, lively

Rallentando (rall.) – gradually getting slower

Ritardando – gradually held back, slower

Poco ritenuto (rit.) – a little held back

Accelerando (accel.) – gradually getting faster

UNIT EIGHT

New Note A

A Finger Puzzle

PW

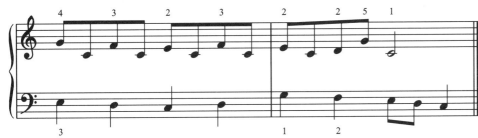

A-mazing Grace

An Upbeat

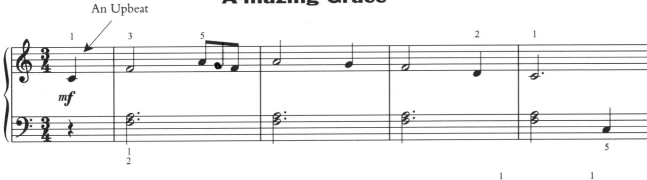

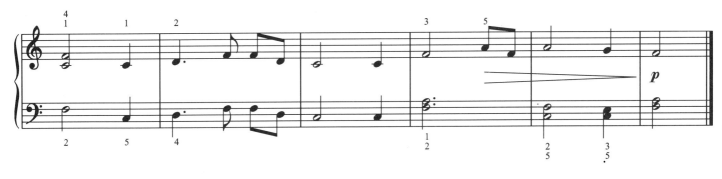

A curved line under a group of notes is called a phrase mark. Try to play all the notes covered by it as if you were singing them in one breath.

Down Yonder Dale

A Courtly Dance

Adding Chord IV

Chord IV in C major uses F A C.
We are using it with C at the bottom.

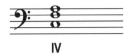

Hot Chord Warm-up

A tune you may know

Michael, Row the Boat Ashore

Spiritual

Strengthen your Fingers!

Play-it-Again Sam's Fingers Together Puzzles

No. 1

Join together – no gaps!

Preparation for No. 2

Right Hand

Left Hand

Both hands together

No. 2

Interlude

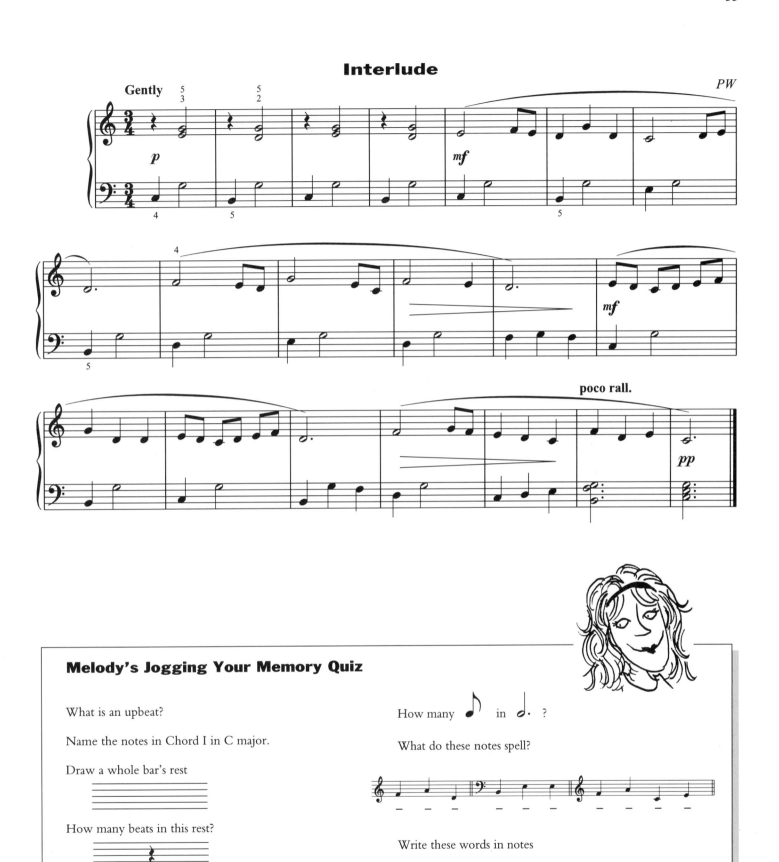

Melody's Jogging Your Memory Quiz

What is an upbeat?

Name the notes in Chord I in C major.

Draw a whole bar's rest

How many beats in this rest?

What does Allegro mean?

What does Rallentando mean?

How many ♪ in 𝅗𝅥. ?

What do these notes spell?

Write these words in notes

B A G G E D   A G E D   D E A D   C A B B A G E

Sharps, Flats and Naturals

Sharp ♯

This sign placed in front of a note tells you to play the next key to the **right**, usually a black note

Flat ♭

This sign placed in front of a note tells you to play the next key to the **left**, usually a black note

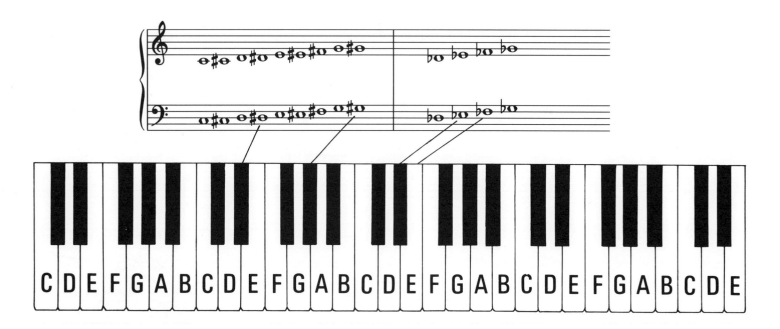

You will notice that all the black notes have two different names, e.g. C♯ = D♭ and so on. Find some more examples. The white notes can have two names as well, e.g. E = F♭

The Natural ♮

This sign cancels a sharp or a flat. Play the white note instead.

Hot Fingers Sharps, Flats and Naturals

No. 1

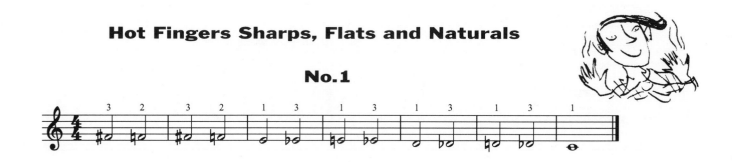

No.2

Try to learn this one by heart!

No.3

Sharpen Up!

Key Signatures

The piece above could have been written with the **key signature** of G major

at the beginning of every set of staves. That indicates that all the Fs are F♯s.

The key signature of F major

indicates that all the Bs in a piece are B♭s.

Key signatures are a kind of musical shorthand, to save writing lots of sharps or flats.

Flats and sharps which occur during a piece (that is, not in the key signature), plus all natural signs, are called **accidentals**. They apply only to the note they are in front of, plus any more notes in that space or on that line for the remainder of the bar. Look at the fourth bar/measure from the end of *Sharpen Up!*. The second F doesn't need a ♯ because it is in the same space as the first F♯. But the next F does need a sharp because it is in a new bar.

Finger Puzzle

For the next piece (*Strange Encounter*), the left hand needs lots of preparation. Try these finger puzzles before you begin, practising each one many times.

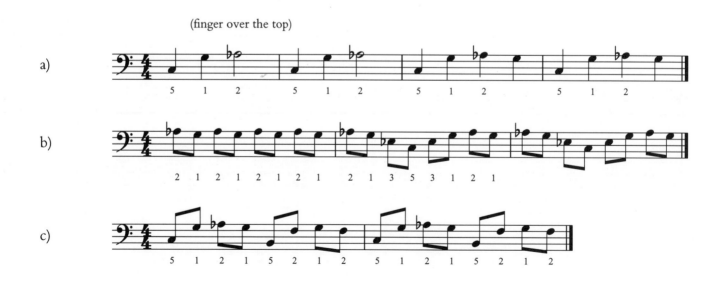

Strange Encounter

PW

Serenade in Flats

PW

REMINDER An accidental at the beginning of the bar affects all others on that line or space, in the same bar.

UNIT TEN

Play-it-Again Sam's
Syncopated Rhythms

In the following tunes you will discover syncopated rhythms. Try these exercises before you start:

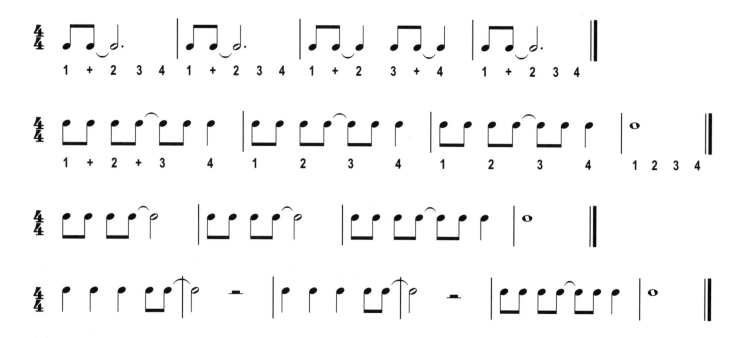

Repeat Signs

When we want a passage to be repeated we use these signs:

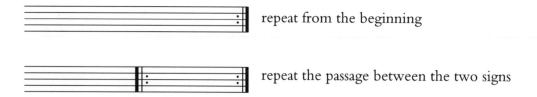

repeat from the beginning

repeat the passage between the two signs

Sometimes when a passage is repeated, the end needs to be different, in which case we use these signs:

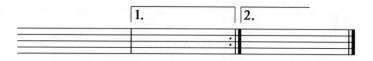

The first time through, play all the music under the $\boxed{1.}$ sign;

but when you play the passage again, leave the $\boxed{1.}$ music out and play from $\boxed{2.}$ instead.

There are examples of these **first–** and **second–time bars** in the next piece.

Walking Bass Blues

> = accent the note

TREMELO
or wobble for
a RAGTIME
EFFECT

Go-for-it Rag Try-Outs

Foot-Tapper Try-Outs

Go-for-it Rag

PW

In ragtime - not fast

Foot-Tapper

tap your foot

Melody's Not-so-Quick Quiz

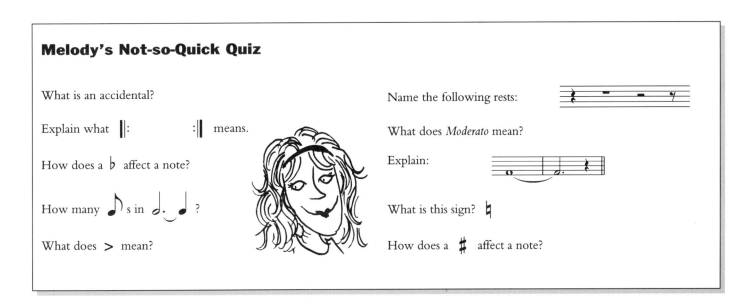

What is an accidental?

Explain what ‖: :‖ means.

How does a ♭ affect a note?

How many ♪s in 𝅗𝅥. 𝅘𝅥 ?

What does > mean?

Name the following rests:

What does *Moderato* mean?

Explain:

What is this sign? ♮

How does a ♯ affect a note?

F major Position

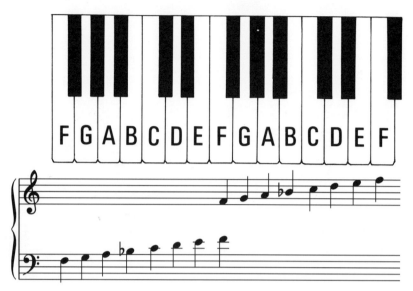

In F major all Bs are B♭s, which is shown by the key signature

Hot Fingers in F

Hot Finger Warm-Ups

Name the Note Test

The Long and the Short of It

Legato

The notes should be played smoothly, usually indicated by a slur

Staccato

A dot placed under or over a note makes it short and separated

Common Time

The time signature **C** (sometimes called Common Time) means exactly the same as $\frac{4}{4}$, that is, 4 crotchet/quarter note beats to the bar.

Play firmly with a loose wrist!

Staccato Stomp 1

Staccato Stomp 2

Legato Lilt

PW

Join together smoothly. The A♭s in this piece are **accidentals**

Tunes you may know

Largo

(Theme from second movement of the 'New World' Symphony)

Dvořák

45

Andante (adapted from Symphony No.94)

Haydn

Melody's Moderato Quiz

What is the key signature of F major?

Write the correct key signature in the treble and bass clefs:

Name these notes:

Find them on the keyboard - **quickly!**

Primary Chords in F major

You played chords I, IV and V^7 in C major in Unit 7. Here they are in F major:

Chord I (F) uses the notes F A C
Chord IV (B♭) uses the notes B♭ D F
Chord V^7 (C^7) uses the notes C E G B♭ (G can be omitted)

Hot Chord Warm-Up 1

Practise this chord progression in F major. Play by 'feel' without looking at your hands.

Hot Chord Warm-Up 2

Lazy Bones

Spreading the accompanying chords

Play-it-Again Sam's Mini Waltz

PW

Hot Chord Warm-Up 3

Forgotten Dreams
(Adding an extra flat or two)

PW

Pause (fermata)

When you see this sign, 𝄐 hold the notes on longer.

More fast terms

Presto – very fast
Allegro vivace – fast and lively
Allegro moderato – moderately fast

More slow terms

Lento – slowly
Adagio – slow, leisurely
Largo – very slow and broad
Andante – quite slow, at a walking speed

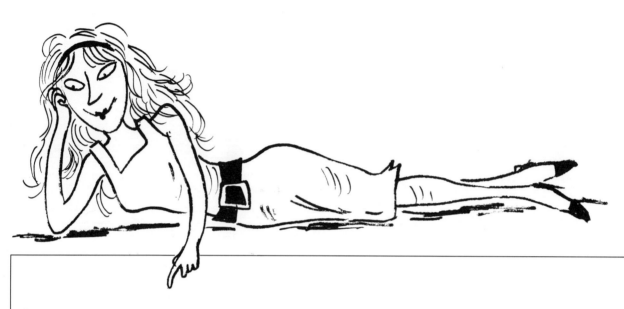

Melody's Mega Quiz

What does *staccato* mean?

What is an up-beat?

What does this time-signature **C** mean?

What does *legato* mean?

What does *Allegro moderato* mean?

Write these words in notes:

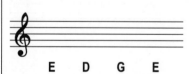

E   D   G   E

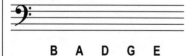

B   A   D   G   E

What does **ff** mean?

What does **pp** mean?

What does **mf** mean?

What is this rest ▬ worth?

What is this rest ⅞ worth?

Name the notes in chord I in C

What does this sign 𝆏 mean?

What does this sign ◁═══ mean?

Name the notes in chord V^7 in F major

What does this sign ♮ do?

G major Positions

This is the key-signature of G major

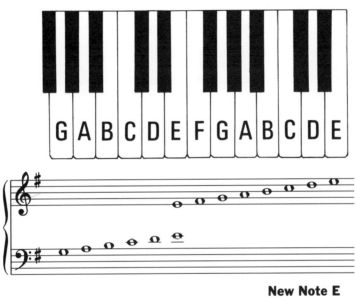

New Note E

Hot Fingers in G

The semiquaver (sixteenth note) is worth ¼ count.

♪ = ¼ count   ♫ = ½ count   ♬♬ = 1 count

Get those hot little fingers movin'! Think of your hand position!

Play as fast as possible.
1st time f = loud
2nd time p = soft

Hot Finger Warm-Up 1

Hot Finger Warm-Up 2

As fast as possible

Semi-detached Rag

PW

The Never-Too-Late-to-Learn Speedometer

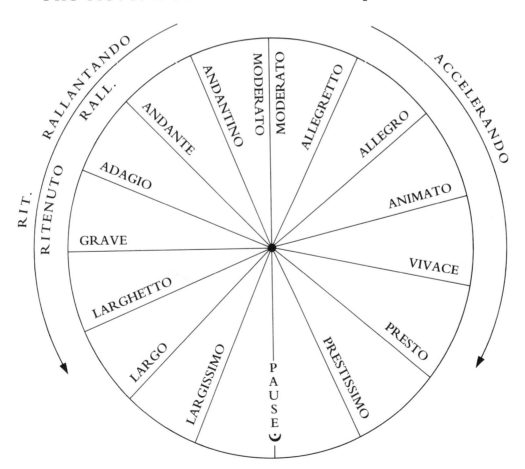

Primary Chords
in G major

Tonic   Subdominant Dominant 7th

Hot Chord Warm-Up in G major

Practise this chord progression in G major:

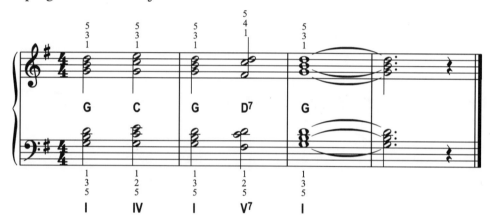

Hot Chord Warm-Up 2

Remember When

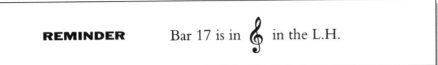

REMINDER   Bar 17 is in 𝄞 in the L.H.

PW

La cì darem la mano

(Duet from Don Giovanni)

Mozart

Moderato

FINE

Da Capo al FINE

Da Capo (D.C.) al Fine means 'repeat from the beginning until you reach **Fine** (the end)'

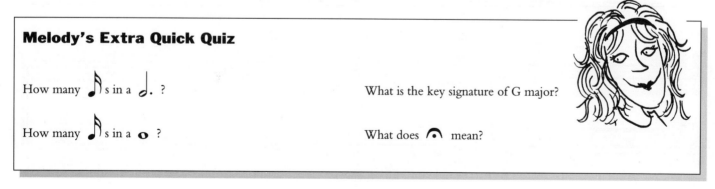

Melody's Extra Quick Quiz

How many ♪s in a 𝅗𝅥. ?

What is the key signature of G major?

How many ♪s in a 𝅝 ?

What does 𝄐 mean?

Dotted Quaver

Dotted Quaver (eighth note) followed by a semiquaver (sixteenth note)

This dotted quaver/eighth note equals three semiquavers/sixteenth notes

Play-it-Again Sam's Rhythm Test

Clap these rhythms:

Clap, then play:

Right Hand

Left Hand

Workouts using

2.

G-Whiz

In a relaxed tempo

PW

FINE

D.C. al FINE

What Shall We Do With The Drunken Sailor?

Jolly

Trad.

Melody's Quite Quick Quiz

What is the key signature of F major?

What is the key signature of G major?

What does *Andante* mean?

What does *Largo* mean?

How many ♪s in a 𝅝 ?

Add these notes together

How many beats?

Name the notes:

Triplets

Introducing the Triplet Rhythm – a group of three notes played in the time of two of the same kind

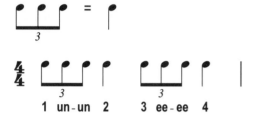

Play-it-Again Sam Rhythms

Clap:

Triplet Warm-Up 1

Triplet Warm-Up 2

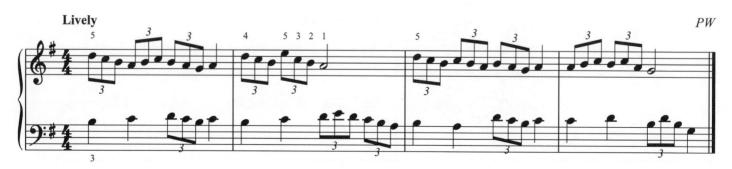

In *Triplet Boogie* we use this movement in the bass. Learn it by heart.

Triplet Boogie

In Boogie style

PW

Oh Yeah!

UNIT SEVENTEEN

New Time Signature

$\frac{6}{8}$ means six quavers to each bar/measure

Clap these rhythms:

Clap then play: **Play-it-Again Sam Rhythms**

Hot Fingers $\begin{smallmatrix}6\\8\end{smallmatrix}$ Warm-Up

Think two dotted crotchets $\left.\right._{\textstyle .}^{\textstyle \rfloor}$ in the bar

> REMEMBER > = accent

The Lincolnshire Poacher

Gaily

Better Late Than Never!

Swing tempo

PW

Printed by
Halstan & Co. Ltd., Amersham, Bucks., England